LEO HO

2016

LISA LAZULI

Lisa Lazuli is the author of the amazon bestseller

HOROSCOPE 2014: ASTROLOGY and NUMEROLOGY HOROSCOPES

And

HOROSCOPE 2015: Astrology and Numerology Horoscopes

Those who enjoy Astrology may all gain insights from my book

NUMEROLOGY DECIPHERED

ABOUT THE AUTHOR

Lisa Lazuli studied astrology with the Faculty of Astrological Studies in London.

She has practised since 1999.

Lisa has been a regular guest on BBWM and BBC Shropshire talking about astrology and doing both horoscopes and live readings. She has also made guest appearances on Fox FM, BBC Cambridgeshire, BBC Northamptonshire, BBC Coventry and Warwickshire and US Internet Radio Shows including the Debra Clement Show.

Lisa wrote horoscopes for Asian Woman Magazine.

Now available:

TAURUS: Your Day, Your Decan, Your Sign

The most REVEALING book on The Bull yet.

and

GEMINI: Your Day, Your Decan, Your Sign

A stunning insight into the Twins

Lisa Lazuli is also the author of

The mystery/thrillers:

A Sealed Fate

Holly Leaves

Next of Sin

As well as:

ARIES HOROSCOPE 2016

TAURUS HOROSCOPE 2016

GEMINI HOROSCOPE 2016

CANCER HOROSCOPE 2016

Delicious, Nutritious Recipes for the Time and Cash Strapped

Paleo Diet: Get Started, Get Motivated, Feel Great.

99 ACE Places to Promote Your Book

Pressure Cooking Reinvented.

Sugar Free Desserts with Pazaz

Sugar-Free Cakes, Cookies, Muffins and Tarts: Sugar-Free Cakes, Cookies, Muffins and Tarts

Depression Busters – The diet to get you on the road to better mental health

Alternative Medicine for Pets: Your Guide to Holistic Health for your Dog and Cat

FOREWARD

Dear Reader,

I hope my yearly horoscope for Leo will provide you with some insightful guidance during what is a very tricky time astrologically speaking, with the heavy planets i.e. Pluto and Uranus at loggerheads in cardinal signs, and Neptune in Pisces calling us all to get in touch with our spiritual side.

I have a conversational style of writing, please excuse any grammatical errors, I write much as I would speak.

As the song goes, "Nobody said it was easy". I know the mass media pump out shows aplenty about quick fix love, money, fame and success; however, life is a journey filled with challenges and obstacles designed to encourage us to find out what we are made of and who we really are.

Embrace the good and bad and enjoy what your unique experience is.

Be the hero in your own personal life movie and never hide your spotlight.

I must add that the best astrology insights are gained from a unique chart based on your time, date, year and place of birth.

If you would like your natal chart calculated for FREE:

Please click below and fill in your DOB on the contact form:

http://lisalazuli.com/2014/06/30/would-you-like-to-know-where-all-your-planets-are-free-natal-chart/

Please join me on Facebook:

https://www.facebook.com/pages/Lisa-Lazuli-Astrologer/192000594298158

Contents

2016 OVERVIEW

The first two-thirds of this year are ideal for Leo; you are able to shine and show the world what you are made of. It is as if the stage has been set just for you, and your unique talents and attributes can come to the fore in every walk of your life. This is an expansive and energetic period when you have the confidence in your intellectual and personality skills to grab opportunities and to let your voice be heard. This is a period in which you are able to accept yourself and when you feel very comfortable with who you are, and this means you have an inner peace and contentment which allow you to make choices that are totally in tune with your destiny. Recognition and acclaim will come your way, and your life will open up to enable you to grow. This is not a time when you feel restricted or inhibited – it seems like you are on the crest of a wave, and your biggest problem may be the fact that you are enjoying yourself too much to make productive use of everything on offer.

This year is excellent for health and recuperation. You will be stronger physically and more vital and will thus be able to achieve more. You may put on some weight, not because you are eating excessively, but because you are more relaxed and are enjoying life.

Leo are not always typically Leo, as shyness is very much part of Leo and many only blossom later in life when they come out of themselves and assume the limelight in terms of leadership or before the public. This is a year when the shy Leo, the Leo who are still waiting backstage can finally take to the stage or connect with their power to lead and to create. This year is wonderful for finding and exploring creative abilities and pursuing courses in subjects like drama, modelling, design, or you may be teaching these subjects instead.

2016 (especially from Jan to July) is an ideal time for planning a big event – this may be a wedding, a launch for your business, a stage production that you are going to take on the road, a welcome home parade, charity drives, fetes or a political rally. Things which you arrange or coordinate will be even more successful if the goal has far-reaching effects, i.e. raising money, raising awareness or education via entertainment. Any promotional event can gather steam and be even more successful than you imagined.

This is an achievement year; leisure is not the overriding theme, commitment to goals and mental resilience is a key attribute, and you will drive forward undeterred to get to where you want to be.

While this year is one that is full of promise and will be one you look back on fondly, you should not allow yourself to take the easy way out and waste money or resources just because you feel invincible. You should make the most of all the business and material benefits this year offers while never forgetting that personal growth and your own evolvement is also an exciting by-product.

Involvement in committees (i.e. parent teacher or the town/city council) may be an avenue you want to go down – it can open the doors to more leadership roles and a greater chance to influence things in your community. If you are in business, you may want to join the local chamber of commerce.

If you are engaged and have been holding off marriage, this is the year to go for it – especially in the spring. It is a highly favourable time to tie the knot. Those of you who are married may want to take a once in a lifetime trip and renew your vows. This also bodes well for 2nd marriages later in life.

2016 is excellent for those of you who like to spread ideas; this may be via teaching, writing or lecturing – ideas that are progressive socially and also those ideas and concepts involving self-help. If you write on and do workshops on positive thinking, religion, personal growth or spirituality, you can be very successful.

2016 is a breakthrough year when you can finally move away from something that has dogged you for many years. It is a time when someone will come into your life and will introduce you to something new – this could be a form of exercise, a diet, a self-help technique, a relaxation technique or a therapy, which can finally free you of a condition or ailment you have had for a long while. Not only can this therapy/diet help you, you may well go on to become an expert in it and either teach or administer it yourself. 2016 is all about more freedom and not being held back, but it's also about passing on knowledge and helping others from your experiences.

While things are going your way this year, you should not wait for things to fall into your lap – you must work hard for it and show that you deserve it. Good karma comes back to you, but only when you give it a chance by initiating – laziness is unfortunately a part of this year, and you should guard against being passive.

This is not a year when you can manage with confinement – it will be highly frustrating for you if you have to tow the line and operate within a tight structure. You will have to find ways of getting more freedom in every aspect of your life and finding ways to express yourself creatively and in terms of leadership. This is a year to push for a leadership role within your current position. If you have been tied down especially over the past two years, this is a time when you will be released from those people or circumstances that tied you down.

This is a time when you can enjoy yourself, make new friends and business contacts and enjoy yourself socially. If you are a person who values spiritual growth, then this is a time when you will be presented with many opportunities to expand your self-awareness, improve your attitude and embrace new aspects of your personality. This is also a wonderful year for discovering talents that have remained latent – you may volunteer for something or get roped into something and quite by accident discover that you are very good at something you have not tried before.

This year Leo are bound to be involved in large scale cultural and scientific advancement; in fact, you could be instrumental in some of the exciting movements ongoing right now, i.e. cultural integration due to mass migration; the development of new financial systems (after the 'failure' of capitalism and socialism) and a new world with borderless societies. The indication is that Leo is at the forefront of developments that will shape and change society for generations to come – you may work on it, lead or write about it, but you are where it's at. Leos in business need to think about the cashless society and how that may change your workplace or business, even your personal life. Leos in the arts may be dealing with the way the digital storage and transfer of music, books or films has made it cheaper to distribute but harder to protect – you may be involved in these changes (from a legal or production point of view) or in the Indie music and publishing industry that has opened up because of these changes. Leos in business may be adjusting to the gradual shift in power from the US to the Berlin-Beijing axis.

You have good organisational and managerial skills that can aid you in starting a business, expanding your business or seeking a more challenging role in your company. This is an excellent year for all jobs that require physicality and physical skills, i.e. sports or manual jobs that need skill and precision. This is also a great year for training in the use of machinery or specialised tools – thus ideal for those learning trades.

2016 is an excellent one for organising others – you have the ability to harness the energy of a group and coordinate and direct team efforts to a successful conclusion. This year can be a very fulfilling one for those of you in jobs like the police where you need good relations with the community to police well – in local government and law enforcement you are able to be more effective due to respect you earn by a fair and broad-minded approach.

This is an impulsive year, and one where you may lash out and act unpredictably, especially when you feel backed into a corner. Your big advantage is the element of surprise; you may put all your plans in place in great secret and suddenly spring your plan on others. You need to be careful of acting in temper as when angered this year (and you do have a short fuse at times) you can act rather self destructively – you may throw something down the drain just to make a point, and you will regret that later. Your challenge is to channel anger and aggression more productively.

Some problems can stem from your association with groups, societies or movements – they may place unrealistic restrictions on you, i.e. you may leave a charity you are involved in as they will not allow you to tweet, or maybe you leave a political party as you disagree with their new direction; you may even disagree with the way your union is representing you; either way, you may disengage from these associations and go it alone or form new ones.

The first two-thirds of the year are the best for planning, execution, financial decisions and contract negotiations; the last third of the year is best for creative input, artistic work, public relations, human resource development and work in the virtual realm. From the fall, you are able to use you sensitivity, humanity and intuition to great effect, but you will tend to be less organised and rather unsystematic; you may also not be as sharp with financial deals. You are highly perceptive this year and yet, in the first part you can act too quickly; later in the year, you are able to harness your feelings and act with better timing. You have good fortune from your ability to sense and go with prevailing events; instinctively taking advantage of trends. Try not to jump on any bandwagon just for the sake of it as you need to judge which trends are going somewhere and which are dead donkeys.

You can have great success in dealing with women this year, especially if those women are in politics, PR, entertainment or law.

One problem you can have is that your personality dominates your perceptions of reality; you can find it hard to step back and see things from another point of view. You can also get a little immersed in your own horizons. You must beware of taking everything personally, even if it is not meant that way. You can also be very uncompromising and also not very empathetic, but you are assertive.

This is an excellent year for coming into your own or blossoming as a person. 2016 is all about you! If you have felt as though you have lived in some else's shadow or your life has been dedicated to others, then this is a time where you can step into the limelight and take centre stage in your life. I mentioned the words 'immersed in your own horizons' in the last paragraph – it may be that that is just what you need ... to be a touch selfish and all about you.

LIFE

Using specialist skills or inside knowledge can help you get a promotion or land employment – you need to sell yourself and make better use of contacts and areas where you are in the know.

This is an ideal time for financial planning for the year ahead: budgeting and looking for smart ways to save and invest. Being savvy with money pays off; gambles do not.

If you can be disciplined about money, then this can be a good month. Saving and paying down personal debt should be your goal. You need to have money aside for unexpected costs; this is not the time to be living too close to the red line.

You may be considering a lifestyle choice this year, which will mean less money, i.e. going to study, working part-time to spend more time with children, changing to a less stressful lower paid job to improve your health or taking time off to go travelling. In any case, you may make a very important choice that will mean getting by on less money, but radically improving quality of life. It is a matter of what really counts to you: money or more fulfilment and less stress.

This month is one where you can get to the bottom of health problems – it is a good time for any type of health testing or allergy testing. If you have been using creams and maybe painkillers to dull down symptoms, then this is a time when you can identify and address the root causes, thereby moving from a cure focus to a prevention focus. You need to be more open to what is causing your health issues from a psychological, pathological and dietary perspective to be able to acknowledge when you and you alone can take action and make changes.

A new therapy or treatment may mean you can resolve a muscular, cartilage or bone-related problem, thereby giving you new freedom and lease on life.

January is a very good time for any Leo who wants to dramatically change their lifestyle, i.e. becoming a vegan or taking up a brand new and challenging sport or exercise.

LOVE

In love, your ability to be strong, resolute and loyal is very important right now – you will have to be the rock, and to a degree you will have to keep a lid on your own emotions and be tough to provide direction in the relationship and support for your partner.

Values are very important to you right now, and you will be firm on setting an example to your children via the way you and your partner communicate, resolve issues and react to problems. You will want to show your children the virtues of being generous and giving, especially to those beyond your social circle.

Differing priorities in your relationship can cause conflict – but you will be determined to impose your value system on your other half. Differing values can also cause disagreements about where to spend and where to save money.

Money is a bone of contention – it may be that one of you is very money driven and the other cares more about happiness; money and how you both feel about it can drive a wedge between you. It is this important to try and find common ground in terms of your approach to materialism.

Single Leo who are dating may distance themselves or break up with people they deem as mean, uncharitable or overly materialistic.

CAREER

Work in fields of advanced technologies or nuclear technologies is favoured. This is an excellent month for those beginning careers in radiography or where sonar and imaging technologies are involved.

This is also a very exciting month for those who do research or study in the areas of space science or even UFOs and unexplained phenomena.

There will be many changes at work in terms of new systems, new locations, new technology; this can cause a great deal of upheaval and changes in terms of the power structure at work. You may have a change in management or a new boss, or perhaps you have to report to a new line manager who works very differently from before. This can complicate your daily routine, and you will have to be flexible – adapting quickly and being prepared to learn the new ways fast can earn you respect and get you noticed.

Bad investment decisions in business will have to be acknowledged and dealt with this month. You really need to be honest with yourself about what is working and what is not in terms of product lines or services you offer. It may be time to prune back in terms of your business and concentrate on core skills and competencies.

This is a challenging month in all money matters and clients may be slow to pay you, and so be careful who you extend credit to and do not count on any money until you have it.

LIFE

This is a very good month for any projects that require you to work alone or in seclusion. It is ideal for writing retreats, locking yourself away to hammer out the last draft of a manuscript or academic paper, actors seeking a quiet spot to learn lines or simply getting to grips with an important personal goal without interruption. You will want to focus and will not welcome interruptions. In most matters you must work to your own initiative as others will simply not understand what you are doing and why it matters. It is a time for deeply personal goals, goals which are highly individual and unique to you.

This is also a great month for surprise parties that require extensive planning and must be done 'top secret'.

February is a very successful time for those of you who compete to entertain – this can mean sportspeople who compete and entertain at the same time or maybe contestants in a quiz or talent show where you are in a competition for your own sake and also for the sake of entertaining.

Relations with authority figures including parents can be strained – you may want their advice and support, but you may resent any interference or control. Sometimes asking advice invites control, and so perhaps you should hold back on asking advice.

LOVE

The love light may not be burning bright on Valentine's Day, but be a little patient as Cupid is not very punctual, and the end of the month will be really excellent for new and old romances.

Leos are feeling good about themselves in Feb and are radiating an inner confidence.

Late February is both harmonious and exciting love-wise. A new romantic partner can open your world to new experiences, and for established couples, your social life will be more exciting. A forgiving, generous and open attitude can help new relationships to develop quickly and with greater meaning within your interactions.

If you have been together for a long time, then this Feb may be the time you finally tie the knot.

Relationships where you grow together and look to the future as a couple will thrive right now, but if you tend to be a couple who harp on old issues and struggle to bury the hatchets, then you can have a hard time now bickering and backbiting, and you may drift apart.

CAREER

You may be working in an office where the left hand does not know what the right hand is doing. Events can be confusing, and the hidden agendas of others may mean that while you are doing the best you can, you are still being undermined. However, if you can stay focused despite others and despite the chaos, then this is a good time for advancement and recognition.

When it comes to criticism, you can be very vulnerable and may be deeply wounded and demoralised by sharp and unfair criticism – even constructive criticism can seem to hit you hard, and the best thing is to take yourself off and surround yourself with things that comfort you and people where you feel protected. You should retreat and switch off totally from the activity where you received the criticism until you have gathered yourself and feel strong enough to determine what was valuable criticism and what was not, and where you want to take things. It is best to think before you react as you may react with emotion and not in a way that is ultimately helpful.

This month is a productive one for public relations, industrial relations and contract negotiations with regular trading partners.

Mentally you are very competitive this month, and so it is a good time for debate, but you will have to ensure you do not go overboard and become argumentative. You will struggle not to get heated when contending with differing views.

You may lack patience right now and so work with children can prove stressful and demanding – you may find it hard to control them and cater for their demands. For teachers, childminders and parents, children can prove very trying, and they will push your limits – you may have an easier time if you give in, but that may set a dangerous precedent.

LIFE

You should embrace the unexpected this month; Leo are a fixed sign and that means that you value constancy and enjoy stability to a point. This month, the things you rely on can undergo change, and this may arouse insecurities within you, throwing you off balance; you should see this as a time to kick away superficial crutches that you have relied upon, perhaps unnecessarily. This is also a good time to consolidate – i.e. get rid of clothes, shoes, power tools, books, etc. You may even raise some money via a sale.

This is also a good month to save money by use of bundle deals, i.e. getting TV, phone, internet as part of one deal; getting a family cell phone contract; holidaying in a group, etc.

This month you need to take your foot off the gas – the temptation is to keep your foot on the gas and go hell for tilt forward to achieve your aims, but this may not necessarily get you anywhere. Something, i.e. a cold, a technical breakdown, severe weather, etc., may stop you in your tracks. This can be a valuable thing, as while you wait for the cold/weather situation to pass, you may get a new perspective you have totally missed before, which will help you to be more effective when you get started again.

LOVE

Relationships mean letting go this month. Especially in new relationships; you may have to let something go to move forward with the relationship – i.e. deciding which of you will give up their flat so you can move in together; your partner may demand that you lessen ties with former boy/girlfriends who you still have good relationships with; there may be issues to do with religion as well. These issues will challenge you to work out exactly how far you will go for this relationship – what you will give up and where the lines are. It can be a revealing phase in your life, and it will force you to analyse what really does matter deep down and where you are not prepared to compromise. There may be circumstances where you need to choose between your family or a parent and your new partner – we cannot be all things to all people, and yet sometimes those close want a big piece of us. We only have so much time, and so it can be a diplomatic exercise moving your attention away from one person to another, especially when you are in a new relationship.

Control and power issues will also arise in all relationships, both new and old, and you need to find different ways of dealing with them – more maturity and understanding of the core psychology is needed.

It can be testing to merge your values, and at times you can be miles apart in terms of your approach – you may need to be more accepting of your partner's views and moral attitudes. This is most difficult when children are involved or even finances as you both have very different priorities. You need to start a new page in terms of how you deal with these issues – perhaps an ongoing discussion rather than acting behind each other's backs. Be upfront, do not conceal your views, and try not to force for your own way at all costs.

If your sex life has become mechanical and unfulfilling, this is a month when you can turn that around and reignite a spark and some excitement; there is more passion and feeling in relationships right now, and conflict can actually be the gateway to better understanding and better sex.

The deeper side of relationships cannot be ignored, and so contentious issues will surface and will demand your attention – the trick is looking at old problems with a new perspective and taking them forward, not being dragged into the same old arguments.

CAREER

March is great for raising money for business investment, getting loan extensions or transferring loans to a new bank. There will be an injection of cash into your business from an outside source. It is a good time to apply for sponsorship, a scholarship or a grant. Money will be available, especially if you are busy with a new venture or project.

March is really excellent for the entertainment, hospitality and sporting industries – especially the last part of March. This is a good time to expand, advertise, run promotions or apply for a listing, i.e. AA rating or encourage good reviews.

This is a much better month than February in all activities to do with children and young people. Businesses focused on welfare and expanding the minds of youngsters should thrive. If you run summer camps or youth centres, these activities should gain attention, and you may even gain publicity in the press.

March favours all careers where you use your personality and ability to entertain – this includes teachers, preachers and sales people, along with traditional forms of entertainment. You need to focus on conveying your message in new and creative ways to grab and keep attention – you can be successful no matter what you are saying/selling as long as you can keep your audience's attention, and so pay great attention in all your presentations to the excitement favour.

You are extremely competitive this month, which will give you a boost in all situations where you need to act decisively, fast and with self-confidence.

March is very good for patents – this is a favourable time for inventors to apply for patents and sell their ideas.

LIFE

Ready to rock the boat? This month it's time for a shake up! Dust off the cobwebs and get out that list of goals. Do you know that writing down goals is a key element in actualising and focusing your attention on what you want? Make sure you spend some time alone this month drawing up a few goals – these can be big or small but should be specific and time constrained. You should write down some specific targets for the next few months, i.e. weight to lose, miles to run, words to write, products to sell, etc. The aim of this is to take advantage of the energy the planets are offering Leo right now for self-actualisation and for personal growth via attainment of goals that matter to you. So often the to-do list is about laundry, errands, bills, groceries that between all of these pressing demands you lose sight of things that make you happy. This is why you need a list of things that you can draw up and an action plan of how to attain and how much time to devote to these important goals in your life. You need to create a clear picture of where you want to be in three months time, and then make sure you have steps you can take that will realistically get you there.

Since there is a strong second house element, money will surely be connected to your goals right now – but it should be more than just saving money, it should be increasing income, getting that promotion or hitting that target. New income streams and new initiatives to earn money via your skills, talents or ability to use social media are indicated right now. Taking on private clients, moonlighting, giving private lessons or getting a franchise can be ways to boost your money – more money may well be the means to achieving other goals.

You are very direct this month and will not don a facade for the sake of keeping anyone happy. As a result, you will make some really solid, supportive new friends who are attracted to who you really are and who click with you.

LOVE

You have a very strong need to express your personality in relationships, and it will be a case of love me for who I am! You are in touch with your true nature and able to present yourself with confidence. If you do have a more dominant partner who has over the years overshadowed you, this is the time when you will come into your own and take more charge in the relationship.

I said before that often Leos are late bloomers; this month you are feeling a change within you, and you feel excited by who you are and how you are evolving – you are also in touch with your sexual nature and your needs sexually.

If you have felt that you are taken for granted in the relationship or that you have to suppress part of your personality, this is the time to change that around and to demand total acceptance. Love is never wanting to change someone, and yet so often in relationships over time we allow people to change us, dampen us down or convince us we are something other than what we believe – right now you feel more in touch with your true nature, and you need your life and your relationships to reflect that. Partners will have to adapt, and this heralds what can be a very exciting rebirth in love relationships. There can be some turbulence in the short run; however, in the long run your strong self image fosters better understanding, deeper meaning and more romance.

This month is a very good month for new relationships – this time in your life is one in which you are most likely to attract someone who appreciates you and can give you what you truly need emotionally. Partly because you understand yourself better.

Deeply manipulative relationships based on control will break down now.

CAREER

Money management and juggling finances is vital in your business – even if you do not inject new cash, you can make the money in your business work harder and go further by changing the way you spend, i.e. short versus long-term financing; outsourcing; making fixed costs variable where possible or maybe reducing time spent on activities with a low ROI. You may want to think up new ways of charging clients or pricing strategies that draw clients in, i.e. loss leaders; freebies or loyalty discounts. You may get more clients by offering flexible payment terms.

Within your personal life, you may be able to make savings by shopping around for your insurance, utility or banking needs – yes, this is boring and tedious, and that is why we tend not to do it and thus lose out on savings that could when added together amount to quite a bit. It may even be worthwhile asking your regular suppliers of phone or other services if any better rates or tariffs are available.

The theme for money and career this month is moderation and security, and so saving, wise investing and better money management is key. Sometimes better money management just means actually thinking more about where you spend – make a monthly chart and see if you can alter expenditure; you may be shocked at how much waste there is.

Creative projects may finally begin to earn you some money this month. This month is also very successful for those who have gone through a very long apprenticeship – this can be in the arts, design, or maybe you have been travelling doing the pub/club scene with your band or act and you finally get the break you want.

This month is also a milestone one for those who are in long financial apprenticeships, i.e. accounting, actuarial or even MBAs.

LIFE

The first two-thirds of this month see Mercury retrograde, and so all communications, training and travel in connection with work can be frustrating, and you may have to go over and correct things many times. The Leo ego is often offended by having to repeat or redo, and so you will have to bottle up that frustration and keep going regardless, as once Mercury goes direct on the 23rd things will take off – ideas in the pipeline will bear fruit, and things you have been learning will finally click in your head.

This month, the focus is on being persistent with your communications – it is about refining ideas, editing and re-editing and getting back to the drawing board until the end result is perfect. In presentations and reports you write, make sure you have not missed out any essential information and check things over diligently.

This is a very sociable month, and you will enjoy many parties and events. Spending on clothing or even jewellery is probable – you are feeling good about yourself and this can extend to needing a new wardrobe to express yourself and create a new image. Image is vital to you now – both in business and personal life, and you will want to project the power you are feeling inside.

This month is very exciting for those who collect or who trade in collectable items for pleasure or for money.

LOVE

Romance is very important to you right now – all relationships must have a strong fantasy and imaginative element. You are not willing to talk about or debate any issues with your partner; you would rather snuggle up, get cozy, have a glass of wine and enjoy time together.

Children and parenting is very rewarding right now, and events to do with your children can bring you and your partner together.

Diplomacy is the name of the game in love – you will shy away from confrontation or excessive communication and agree to disagree or at least put out the olive branch to smooth things over. This is not about being a doormat or a yes-person, it's about picking your battles and not making a big issue about things of marginal concern.

This is a time when you can use your charms to get favours from the opposite sex – make sure you do not lead anyone on.

CAREER

Planning in careers is very important – you need to think more clearly about where you are and if you are getting where you want to be. Focus on your career strategy and start looking for new prospects within you current firm or even elsewhere. This is a good month for career-related training to enhance skills and improve chances of promotion.

This is a much better month financially, and you will have more leeway in terms of money available for new projects and investment in your infrastructure. This can be a good month to invest in making your business smarter, i.e. better signage, new business cards, new shop layout, better reception area.

May is also excellent for cocktail parties or events to promote new product lines.

Ethics is important in your work, and you may pay more attention to green issues, fair trade policies and equal opportunities – you might even offer an apprenticeship or sponsor a young person in their vocational training. Making your business more green may make you eligible for a tax rebate.

This is a very good month for start-ups, especially in emerging industries or with new concepts, i.e selling via pop-up shops.

A very good month for those of you who write on travel-related topics, i.e. camping, walking holidays, camper vans, backpacking, adventure holidays, etc.

LIFE

This month is one of quite rapid advancement as a result of precious hard work and effort; it can also be a period where things move very fast, so much so that you can suddenly be landed with so much work it's overwhelming. You may be under pressure to make very important and far-reaching decisions. Be careful of the commitments you take on as you are inclined to think anything is possible, and you may underestimate the work involved down the line. Do not promise more than you can deliver.

As a woman, you will be able to relate to men more easily, and men will have better relations with superiors. This month is one where you can deal with bureaucracy and red tape effectively, especially when they are to do with compliance with rules, regulations and laws. June is excellent for applications for business rights, licences or acceptance to a university course.

This is a very productive time, and you can work very effectively and efficiently. Work done with other cultures or involving travel is very lucrative, especially if it involves education or promoting human rights and opportunities for the underprivileged. You may well assume a role of leadership in a charitable or voluntary initiative. This month is really fulfilling for those of you who work in large multinational organisations like the UN, Medicine Sans Fronteirs, Red Cross, Save the Children, etc.

Home life can be hectic and chaotic this month, and breakdowns or malfunctions can waste time and cause frustration. There may be arguments about home improvements, where to move or if to move.

In cases where you live with your parents, there can be independence issues where you have to fight to get your needs and voice appreciated. There may also be boundary issues, where you have to let your folks know when they have to back off – with more and more adults living with their parents due to city property prices, these issues are now more common.

LOVE

You tend to be impatient in love this month, and if compliments and affection do not come when you want them to come, you may get angry and turn cold. Leos are rather sulky this month; actually, being sulky is a defence mechanism that you resort to when you feel unloved or vulnerable. Leos may be overreacting a little this month – thus the advice is not to be over-sensitive and look for problems where there are none. You may be picking up the wrong signals or jumping to inappropriate conclusions based on a pessimistic take on the situation.

You are working very hard right now and are feeling pressure, and this may spill over into relationships where you tend to act snappy or irritable – you may also have unrealistic expectations from your partner who may struggle to know what you do want and where you are at this month.

You need to be more carefree and relaxed in the relationship sphere – you also need to be more trusting and less reactionary. It may be better to let some things go rather than dwelling on them or going on the slow cooker until you bubble over. There is a tendency to look for things to get angry about as anger is your go-to emotion right now – it may be easier to be angry than to deal with other emotions; ask yourself, however, if it's worth it. This can apply to new and old relationships and is a symptom of stress rather than anything stemming from the actual relationship.

CAREER

Younger people may find opportunities to work or study overseas. This is also a good time for working with, for, or in the public sector – you may gain a lucrative contract or find employment in the public sector. So if you are applying for jobs, do not neglect public sector opportunities.

June is an excellent one for publicity and awareness of ecological and environmental causes. Work in improving the environment and wildlife preservation can be of interest to you, and if you are already involved, you can make advances.

This is a month where you grow by your work – i.e. success in terms of money or promotion can have a substantial effect on your confidence and motivation. Success breeds more success and you work harder and harder as you feel fulfilled and also vilified in terms of your choices. Often in our career we are plagued by 'what if ...' and 'I should have done it differently ...' etc., but this month you sense a universal plan and that you are well on the way to not only success, but also a personal pride in what you have achieved.

Work in general this month has a feel-good factor, and you have a sense that you are doing good in terms of the wider social and spiritual context.

Organisational skills and your ability to co-ordinate teams and get people working together in a structured way is important – you will need to be mentally skilled in terms of how you talk to others and also motivating. Being critical right now can backfire, even if you are within your rights – you need to steer others in the right direction by encouraging them and emphasising what they are doing right, rather than dwelling on the negatives of people's performance. Being diplomatic right now can slow you down and test your patience, but it will yield better results in the long run.

LIFE

There is a subtle change in you this month – you are more adaptable, more open to change and less likely to cling sentimentally to symbols and objects from the past. You are able to sense the subtle changes around you and act long before they occur to lessen their impact. Suddenly changes you were dreading, you will begin to embrace and feel more positive about. Keep your plans flexible as this is the beginning of a period of information flow and new developments. This is not the time to be complacent or demoralised as your perspective can alter dramatically due to overnight changes.

You may find yourself in a new social circle this month, and you may feel like a fish out of water – it may be via work, via a new love partner or because you are in a new neighbourhood, but you will be thrust among people who you may not understand and who may not get you. You will need to hang back for a while and slowly warm them up. Best not to go in all guns blazing with a 'take me as I am' approach – see how they operate and work your way in with consistency.

In all of your ongoing projects, being consistent despite obstacles is an excellent strategy – show your client, your boss or your customers that while everything may change, you will always be solid in terms of service, information and a personable approach.

Leos have so much flair and drive; you love to create and entertain, and yet this month is more about perfecting and refining your skills or your end product. You should not be in a rush to put out new material; the focus should be on polishing up existing material, products, writings or skills. Any insecurity right now can actually drive you to work harder to create a better end product. You should seek out criticism and not shy away from it, as right now some constructive criticism is very helpful.

LOVE

Single Leo are cautious in new romance this month – you will hold back on your feelings and be inclined to take things slowly. This is ideal for new relationships with colleagues or people you meet via your profession; it is also favourable for age gap relationships. Single Leo will gravitate to people who exude a quiet, understated confidence, and who offer an anchor; this is not a very adventurous time in romance, it is time for something that feels safe and solid. Perhaps it is due to the shifting sands in the Leo's life; the subtle yet obvious changes that are taking place, that it is in relationships that you crave stability and constancy.

This is a time when Leo value stability, strength and responsibility in a partner. When you feel secure you are at your most loving, sensual and sexy; however, if you have a trust issue or sense weakness in your partner, you can find it very hard to relax and be intimate.

Leo will not be patient with lovers who are very emotional or attention-seeking – you need them to step up to the plate and be mature, not act like a kid.

Romance needs both commitment and extra effort this month due to a great amount of external pressure on the relationship and on your time – you both need to be mature and sensible about how you deal with external irritants, i.e. ex partners or children. Your partner needs to support, not put additional pressure on you. You must acknowledge the commitments you both have, and both need to make time to nurture each other, rather than taking things out on each other or whinging in an unproductive way.

CAREER

In creative fields, you will be subject to constraints and controls that can make doing your work harder, i.e. less funding, more regulation, union restrictions, etc. – you need that flexible approach to react quickly and find ways around it.

You may have to go for additional training for the purpose of expanding the services you offer or enhancing your business and saving money, i.e. you may be a dancer who gets website creation training to aid you in running your own website and saving costs. Being more self-reliant is a theme, and so any skills you can learn that can save you time and money within your day-to-day work is valuable. This can mean DIY skills, which save you calling in a handyman when things go wrong in your guesthouse or IT skills so that you can fix your own PC and do not lose time while your equipment is down.

Being creative is hard work this month as the juices just are not flowing, and you are not feeling very inspired. This is a time when you go back to techniques and basics to kick start your artistic projects – there is nothing wrong with looking to the past for inspiration and sticking to more tried and trusted themes and methods to get you started.

In all jobs, the management and organisational side as opposed to the marketing, selling, promoting or creative sides is important – you must ensure you operate efficiently and have a systematic approach that ensures nothing gets left undone. In all jobs now there is an element of multitasking, and if you are not organised by nature, something always gets neglected, and so this month you want to ensure you have lists and systems that ensure everything that demands your attention gets it and timeously.

LIFE

Your mind is very sharp right now, and you are excellent at dealing with things that require analysis and critical review. You are in a cautious and serious frame of mind and are able to deal with difficult problems and intense responsibility. This month is ideal for taking on people or tasks that often prove hard to handle – you have more patience and have a dogged mental determination that can keep you calm while you grind out a result. This is not really a month for quick turnabouts and results; if you do begin something new, you must be patient in learning the ropes and laying foundations. Results will come slowly at first.

August is a very good month for those pursuing educational or vocational training goals – this is a good time to apply for placements or begin your studies.

You are capable of being very persuasive and can win people over with attention to detail and information provided. You must be thorough and persistent, and you should not allow colleagues to put you off or distract you.

This is a very good time for playing to your strengths and keeping an even keel no matter what is going on about you – you are the calm person who delivers when others get flustered.

You need to look after your health this month as your body is more stressed and prone to tiredness than usual, so be sure to take vitamins and minerals (especially magnesium and calcium) and eat plenty of fresh fish, fruit, veg and organic meat.

LOVE

You can come across as very sharp and critical this month, and so do not be surprised if your partner has a double take at some of the things you say – you feel as if you are saying it as it is, but you may need to be a little more subtle.

Simplicity is what matters to you in love – you need to get right to the heart of the matter without false pretences and dancing about the key issues. You will not walk on eggshells, and you won't lose your temper either; you will be inclined to state your opinions in a matter-of-fact way without being over-emotional, and this can be very effective.

Sexual attraction is very important in new relationships right now. Chemistry and that instant feeling of interest in a person is what will get love going rather than the friendship first method. New relationships can be very competitive and may even be a little contentious – i.e. you may be fiercely competing against someone at work, and you may not even think you like them and then suddenly, BAM, you find that the tension is all about attraction.

It may be that anger is a defence against passion, i.e. someone who really excites you may enrage you in equal measure. You may almost not want to fall for this person as you know that it will be a very intense relationship, and you are in two minds whether you want that.

Relationships with a good sex life will thrive this month while if you have not been connecting sexually, you may argue and fight and do quite a bit of door slamming and waltzing out in temper. So get your sex life going again, and do not waste all the love, energy, and passion available this month in needless arguing.

Relationships can be strained due to differences about disciplining the children – again, compromise and bridging the gap between differing values is a theme of the year and needs to be worked on consistently and with patience and understanding.

CAREER

An extremely productive and insightful month for those in editing, consulting, data analysis and research. This month is ideal for attention to detail and focus on small print. You are capable of prolonged concentration and focus, and so if you need to take an exam or work to a tight deadline, this is ideal.

Scientific work and publishing of academic papers this month is favoured.

In careers involving manufacturing, there can be delays, late shipments, strikes and equipment breaking down – be aware of this if your deadlines are tight.

Leo have a chance to make an impression by spotting something everyone has missed – this is thus very opportune for those negotiating contracts, in legal proceedings or in criminal matters.

What you cannot do right now is cut corners – you must be diligent and see things through until the end – be careful of delegating work, you will have to check over things thoroughly. In vital business communications, allow time for delays, and be aware that clients may pay more slowly, and so keep an eye on your cash balance as liquidity is vital this month.

LIFE

This is a month of increasing financial security and financial progress. It is a good time to start a new investment plan or open a savings account. Time spent planning your money and thinking about pensions and cost-effective borrowing is time wisely spent. You may be trying to arrange finance for big purchase, i.e. house or car or putting in offers – this is a good time to judge the market and get a really good deal without compromising on quality.

This month is excellent for negotiating in money matters and driving a hard bargain. There is much information to take on right now whether you are investing, learning, buying something complex, etc., and at times you may feel mentally overloaded, but you are able to cope as long as you tackle things systematically, not with a blitz approach.

The pace of this month is very fast, and it can be very good for travelling in connection with conventions, sales or promotional activities. Travel, especially national travel is a feature of your life and can bring you success and enjoyment.

Balance is important right now as you can get carried away on tangents that are not connected to your ultimate goal – keep asking yourself – why am I doing this? Am I spending too long on this? Is this getting me closer to a goal? You may find that certain parts of your life start small and suddenly snowball. Suddenly, you find that they have taken over your time, i.e. you agree to babysit for a friend once and suddenly every weekend is spend babysitting her children. You have to learn where to draw lines in all aspects of your life.

Try and complete on all contracts and financial transactions before Mercury goes retrograde on the 22nd.

LOVE

September is an excellent time for broaching sensitive issues in the relationship as you can come across in a non-threatening and fluent way. You are able to be sensitive to the needs of your partner and yet firm about matters of importance. You are in a very open frame of mind and are willing to try and meet your partner halfway, which is very helpful. This is a month when problems in relationships can be resolved or at least moved forward. It is also a time to recognise that relationships are dynamic and are works in progress, where the ups and downs should be seen as part of the unfolding of a private drama that can be bittersweet yet incredible beautiful. When the Japanese break a vase, they glue it together and keep it on display as they feel the breaks are what make it unique and even more precious – you should also see your relationship as one when difficulties faced and resolved add to the core value and deepen the pleasure of the union. This plays into the theme of growing through love and evolving in your relationships – relationships that are totally stuck and riddled with stubbornness from both sides will struggle this month and this year.

In new relationships, Leo are extremely charming and can make a favourable impression – this is a time when good manners, grace, politeness matter to you, and you will be repelled by any coarse or uncouth behaviour. People will find it easy to relate to and open up to you this month; you are very receptive to emotions and eager to be helpful. Your intelligence and ability to make good conversation will open doors to new love – you may find that you click with someone with similar artistic interests. Love has very much an intellectual side – you are unlikely to be attracted to someone who does not stretch you mentally or does not share your interests. Opposites attract is not the key for Leo this year in love – new romantic partners must be on the same page as you when it comes to likes, mentality, intelligence and a quest for a serious and loving relationship. If lovers just want a passing fling, that will not be for you.

CAREER

A good month to negotiate a higher salary – you may feel that you are undervalued, and it may be time for you to use your leverage as an excellent and productive employee to get more benefits, better pay or more flexible hours. Ask yourself if you are over-qualified or have outgrown your current position – while you may be comfortable and happy where you are, you may well need a change as you are not fulfilling your potential. This is the time to push for a new position.

In self employment, you may need to re-evaluate your charges and make sure that they reflect your expertise, time and costs – it may well be that you are charging too little, almost underselling and are not covering the value of your time. If you run, say a guesthouse, you may be able to save by cutting back on costs that are not an essential selling point, i.e. fresh flowers, free sherry, extra cakes. Ask yourself, what makes a client come to me? Then get rid of peripheral services that cost you time and money and are not really valued by your clients.

This is an excellent month for trade and business with overseas clients.

Be careful in how you organise your month as over-scheduling could have you rushing about feeling out of control. It is likely that one activity will take up a disproportionate amount of your time, and you may have to put more and more resources into that activity to the detriment of others just to keep it going.

LIFE

This is a month when an unexpected event can lead to a chance to escape a situation that had either trapped you or caused you stress. It is almost a 'get out of jail' free card month – a sudden release of pressure or even managing to clutch victory from the jaws of defeat. It is a month of often surprising turnabouts.

If a person has had a hold over you in terms of them holding all the cards in a situation, they may lose their power, and you will have to take your chance; make changes, and make sure they never get that hold again.

There are openings in business, education and career this month; new beginnings in terms of any project that offers financial reward and a chance to get into a position of authority and more power. October is all about more power for you and you being more effective in your life and within your circles – it is about getting your voice heard and standing out from the crowd.

You will make significant progress on long-term goals, and greater status and enhanced standing in your community will come your way. October is very favourable for those of you involved in cultural or religious activities – this can include curators of historic cathedrals or those involved in promoting local tourism or arranging cultural events.

LOVE

Leo are very proactive in romance this month – you are initiators in terms of sex and romance. You are feeling confident and secure in yourself, and this is very attractive. You will feel like spoiling your partner, not only in terms of material things, but in terms of giving massages, making a special meal, etc. This is not a month to let things drift in your love life; extra work you put in and effort in terms of arranging nights out, bringing flowers, making romantic gestures, hiring a babysitter so you have more time alone will go a long way.

It is also a good time to spice up your love life by trying something new – new underwear, new locations, some erotic literature; find ways to help you to be more expressive and relaxed about lovemaking.

Single Leo will again be inclined towards establishing love relationships with people with whom they already have a strong connection; i.e. family friends, work colleagues, neighbours. This is because what is familiar is secure for Leo in 2016 and Leos are less likely to drift far from the social circle when looking for love. Potential partners must offer the Leo affection and consistency. Leo are not after games or love affairs with people who are volatile or unpredictable. Leo are risk averse in love, and so while they want adventure with a partner, they do not want the love affair as such to be a bumpy ride.

CAREER

This month is excellent for those in politics, construction and international relations. If you work in any industry that has an aspect of the above or you work in a related industry, it can be a very productive time.

October will be profitable for any business linked to tourism or culture. In your business, try to link into any local events, especially those to do with religion, culture or local history to piggy back off the marketing done by others and the general vibe. Halloween is the obvious event to link to with themed discounts or marketing on your social media pages or shop window, but do not miss out on any other events.

Where you can do very well this month is in knowing when to push forward and when to hold back – in some areas, you need to edge forward while you keep a close eye on the competition, then edge forward again. This is not the time for a full on onslaught; you need to take a measured approach and keep adjusting as you go, redefining your approach and watching what the others are doing before you play all your cards. Always hold something in reserve right until the end.

Your reputation for honesty and integrity will be instrumental in growing your business or client base by word of mouth – in any decision you make, do not compromise on moral values.

Use your influence within your job to help others in terms of training, offering your experience or helping others to get on the ladder. It is time to see what you do in a wider context – that means you should look for chances to use your skills outside of work in a charitable or community sense.

LIFE

This month, you will consolidate and build on your excellent progress last month. This month you can achieve a great deal of work in quick time without compromising on quality. Things are working together well, and work in teams, individually or with people you coach or teach can be rewarding and productive.

Your health is strong and robust right now, allowing you to achieve more physically as you feel strong. This is a very good time for training and weight-loss exercise; this is also great for those who want to build up to a big challenge fitness-wise. Consistency and regular training will give you the best results; do not have a yo-yo approach where you do a massive amount one day and then slack off – keep going each day. This is an ideal time to take up a new sport.

You are keen to look after yourself in November, and this includes being strict about your sugar and carb intake. If your career involves looking good, i.e. sports, modelling, dance, presenting, beauty sales or therapies, you can make strides in terms of your appearance, i.e. clear skin, toned body, fitter and flatter.

This month your ability to work with children, both your own and others is enhanced – you are able to be strict and keep control while offering them inspiration and fun. Working with children can be very therapeutic for you, and it may help you to regain inspiration for long-lost goals and dreams that had sadly gone by the wayside.

You have a chance right now to co-ordinate young people to use their talents, and at the same time help raise money or aid children less fortunate. Your work with children may come from some activity you already do or may be totally unexpected.

You are strong now, and this strong sense of purpose and sense of self can be used to press forward harder to get your life into shape so you are where you want to be come 2017.

LOVE

A fun month in love as you are spontaneous and contented. You are in for your share of romance and good times – but it is not a teenage kind of romance, it is more mature romance, so it will be sophisticated and not a frenzied, haphazard matter. This month is a perfect one to start appreciating one another again, especially if the stress of life has taken its toll on your relationship, and you have not had as much quality time together as you would have liked.

While single Leo will meet many people now who can influence your life in a positive way for many years to come, romance and a relationship may not blossom right away, i.e. you may meet someone who you click with, but whom is shortly moving overseas for a job. Or it may be that you meet someone now who you are attracted to but with whom you cannot currently have a proper relationship, and he/she is still with someone. Or it may be you who is still not totally finished with your ex. So the month is filled with promise for meeting partners with potential and yet that potential can take a year or so to unfold.

Responsibilities feel lighter now, and so this is a good time to strengthen the emotional and sexual side of relationships.

CAREER

Creative projects can get some reward right now. In creative or artistic pursuits, you may get some help this month in terms of extra pairs of hands that come on board to help you fine tune and finish things up. You may even call in an expert to help you get a project just perfect.

This is also a very good time for critical review, i.e. getting your work looked over closely by a critic, auditor, proofreader or IT specialist, just to be sure that everything is as perfect as it can be.

Right now, perfection counts, and you cannot afford to let your hard work be marred by a small oversight or glitch.

A great time for work parties as you can mix work and pleasure this month without compromising on standards or relationships. The teamwork ethic is great for those of you who work in groups. This is an ideal time for throwing not only staff parties but parties for your suppliers, distributors or anyone who you see as an essential part of your network and day-to-day worklife.

November is great for promotions and marketing, and so get all your Holiday Season literature and copy ready and get it out before December. Do no neglect traditional forms of marketing this month as it is not only about social media and internet based marketing; face-to-face and personal contact as a form of approaching new customers or clients should not be forgotten.

Investments can fair well, as long as you make calculated risks; this is not the time to gamble, but if you invest wisely you can profit.

LIFE

The desire within you burns hot this month – you will do anything to get what you want, and sometimes you can even be obsessive and can lack common sense and moderation. This is a great month for goals that require great persistence and determination, and yet you may actually not be achieving much – these goals may ultimately not be very productive; they may be ego-driven or impulsive. This energy is best used to achieve goals that you will have something to show for, i.e. a purchase to enhance your business or personal life at a great price or a new computer program to expedite your work and save time; however, I foresee that many Leos may waste this energy chasing bargains on goods that appeal only for a short time and possess no long-term usefulness.

This month, you will be forced to focus on things you would prefer to ignore. It is a case of 'if it ain't broke, don't fix it,' but if it is broke or even cracked, fix it without delay and do not make excuses.

Self-honesty is vital right now as in reference to the previous paragraph you may not be being entirely honest with yourself about what needs fixing in your life. It is better if you own up to anything that is not working and attend to it, rather than denying it and being hit by an unpleasant and public revelation of this problem.

This year was about seizing back control in your life and taking back the initiative; this month will test how well you can use that control; will you use it productively, or will you run a bit wild? You have a very strong sense of self, and yet your purpose is somewhat ill-defined. In December, you can have great success and can make an impact on events in your home life, but you must be organised and have clearly defined goals.

Vague goals are a problem now as you do tend to rush off at tangents. Make a plan and stick to it.

LOVE

You can be a little defensive this month, and if you let it go too far, this can lead to belligerence. You need to listen more to the valid points that you partner is making; you may be a little pig-headed about activities that you place value on, and you may not be able to see that perhaps they are not the best use of you time or money. Even when your partner has your best interests at heart, you can struggle to take that advice at heart as it will involve a climbdown. Remember that this month backing off and admitting where you may be wrong can massively improve relations and communications.

Pride can be the biggest problem in relationships, and so if you can make sure that from your side pride does not distort your ability to be logical and compromising, then things can go far better.

This month relationships can grow via confrontation, and yet, if you stand your ground and will not give an inch, then you will just be on a collision course with no chance of learning anything or taking the relationships forward. Some confrontation via conversation is extremely cathartic for your relationship, and you have the opportunity this December to clear the air about any long held anger issue – you can finally get that out the way and have a much better 2017 for it. The key is really listening, not just doing all the talking and expecting to be listened to.

You may well be spending the last Christmas in your current home, and so the memories will be special.

CAREER

You need to be open to input from others and must focus on teamwork. You need to communicate better with your team members and not go off on your own and then suddenly present your work expecting everyone to say, "Wow!" People in your workplace may actually resent you if you work without consulting and keeping others informed of where you are at.

If you are in sales and negotiations this month, you can be skilful at steering conversation in a direction that will suit you and your business. You are also able to engineer circumstances that will open opportunities for you to express your ideas or draw more attention to your work. You should be very conscious of the subtle messages you send out as sometimes you get very caught up in what you are doing, and you can allow your enthusiasm to become a little domineering. So do watch out for the reactions of others and be sensitive to signals they may be giving off that you have gone too far.

If you are a manager of a department or team leader, you can be extremely protective of your staff this season in doing your best to negotiate bonuses and also better conditions and a higher budget for them.

There is quite a bit of anticipation for 2017 within you career as there are many changes pending, and while it may not be clear exactly what is going to happen, you know it is going to be stimulating.

THANK YOU FOR BUYING MY BOOK AND ALL THE VERY BEST FOR 2016 AND 2017

Made in the USA
Middletown, DE
14 November 2015